DETOXING from Gambling

DETOXING FROM ALCOHOL

DETOXING FROM DRUGS

DETOXING FROM GAMBLING

DETOXING FROM SHOPPING

DETOXING FROM SOCIAL MEDIA

DETOXING FROM A
TOXIC RELATIONSHIP

DETOXING FROM
UNHEALTHY EATING HABITS

DETOXING FROM VIDEO GAMES

DETOXING from Gambling

By Jacqueline Havelka

MASON CREST
MIAMI

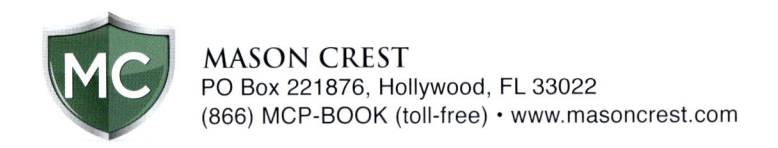

MASON CREST
PO Box 221876, Hollywood, FL 33022
(866) MCP-BOOK (toll-free) • www.masoncrest.com

Copyright © 2023 by Mason Crest, an imprint of National Highlights, Inc. All rights reserved. No part of this publication may be reproduced or transmitted in any form or by any means, electronic or mechanical, including photocopying, recording, taping, or any information storage and retrieval system, without permission in writing from the publisher.

Printed in the United States of America

First printing
9 8 7 6 5 4 3 2 1

Series ISBN: 978-1-4222-4719-8
Hardcover ISBN: 978-1-4222-4723-5
ebook ISBN: 978-1-4222-7094-3

Cataloging-in-Publication Data on file with the Library of Congress

Developed and Produced by National Highlights, Inc.
Editor: Andrew Morkes
Cover and Interior Design: Tara Raymo • CreativelyTara
Layout: Priceless Digital Media, LLC

Publisher's Note: Websites listed in this book were active at the time of publication. The publisher is not responsible for websites that have changed their address or discontinued operation since the date of publication. The publisher reviews and updates the websites each time the book is reprinted.

QR CODES AND LINKS TO THIRD-PARTY CONTENT

You may gain access to certain third-party content ("Third-Party Sites") by scanning and using the QR Codes that appear in this publication (the "QR Codes"). We do not operate or control in any respect any information, products, or services on such Third-Party Sites linked to by us via the QR Codes included in this publication, and we assume no responsibility for any materials you may access using the QR Codes. Your use of the QR Codes may be subject to terms, limitations, or restrictions set forth in the applicable terms of use or otherwise established by the owners of the Third-Party Sites. Our linking to such Third-Party Sites via the QR Codes does not imply an endorsement or sponsorship of such Third-Party Sites or the information, products, or services offered on or through the Third-Party Sites, nor does it imply an endorsement or sponsorship of this publication by the owners of such Third-Party Sites.

CONTENTS

Introduction 7
Chapter 1: **What is a Gambling Addiction?** 11
Chapter 2: **Signs of a Gambling Disorder** 25
Chapter 3: **Consequences of Gambling Addiction** 37
Chapter 4: **Preventing and Treating**
　　　　　　 Gambling Addictions 51
Glossary of Key Terms 70
Further Reading and Internet Resources 74
Index 75
Credits 79
Author's Biography 80

KEY ICONS TO LOOK FOR:

Words to Understand: These words with their easy-to-understand definitions will increase the reader's understanding of the text while building vocabulary skills.

Sidebars: This boxed material within the main text allows readers to build knowledge, gain insights, explore possibilities, and broaden their perspectives by weaving together additional information to provide realistic and holistic perspectives.

Educational Videos: Readers can view videos by scanning our QR codes, providing them with additional educational content to supplement the text. Examples include news coverage, moments in history, speeches, iconic sports moments, and much more!

Text-Dependent Questions: These questions send the reader back to the text for more careful attention to the evidence presented there.

Series Glossary of Key Terms: This back-of-the-book glossary contains terminology used throughout this series. Words found here increase the reader's ability to read and comprehend higher-level books and articles in this field.

6

Introduction

We live in stressful times. The COVID-19 pandemic, political unrest, and other ongoing challenges (such as poverty, racism, serious damage to the environment, job loss, financial distress, and the illnesses and deaths of loved ones) have raised stress to record levels. "These compounding stressors are having real consequences on our minds and bodies," according to the American Psychological Association, which says that these and other problems are causing a "national mental health crisis" in the United States. The situation is the same or even worse in other countries around the world.

As a result, many people are abusing drugs and alcohol more frequently and/or engaging in other addictive behaviors (such as gambling) to reduce stress and blunt the pain of the loss of loved ones, relationships, homes, or jobs, or other serious life events. One example is the rising number of drug overdoses, which have been fueled by the growing use and spread of the deadly opioid fentanyl. Nearly 100,000 Americans died from overdoses from June 2020 to June 2021—an 18.2 percent increase from June 2019 to June 2020, according to the Centers for Disease Control and Prevention. Other addictions—such as problem gambling or spending too much time on social media or playing video games—are not typically physically

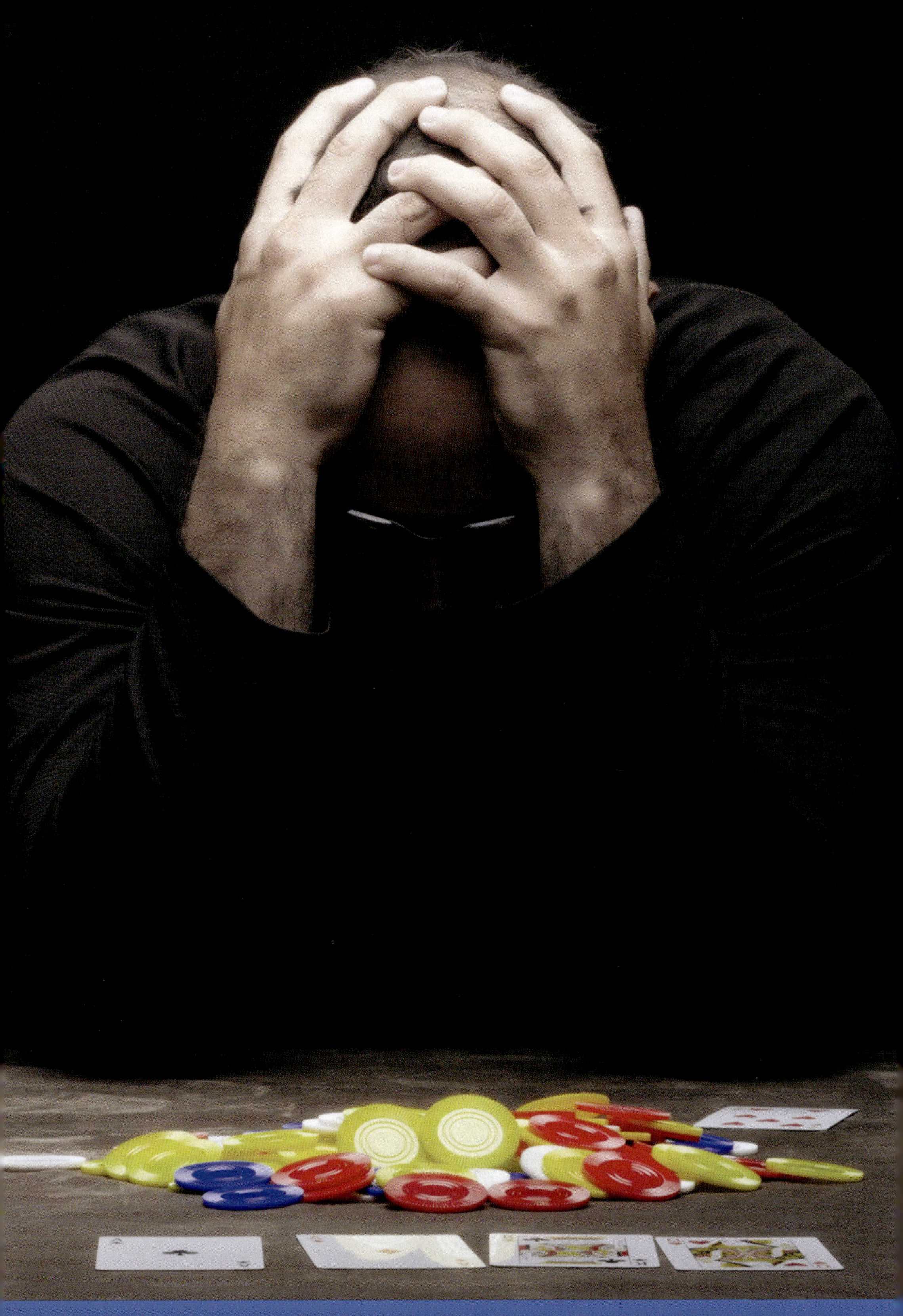

dangerous, but they can damage our mental health, cause us to lose focus on important things in life (e.g., our families, relationships, faith, or careers), and otherwise downgrade the quality of our lives.

For those who are addicted to drugs or alcohol or who have unhealthy relationships with food, gambling, or even shopping or social media, it can seem daunting to overcome these challenges, especially given the ongoing stressors in their lives. But there is hope for anyone who feels that they are controlled by an addiction or who seeks to otherwise re-balance their lives. They will have a bright future if they seek help with their addictions from friends and families, and, most significantly, from counselors, physicians, and clinicians (such as psychologists and psychiatrists).

Each book in the *Detoxing from* series spotlights a major addiction; discusses the negative physical and mental effects of the addiction on the addict, as well as its effects on family and other loved ones; and provides an overview of treatment strategies for the addiction. Stories of those who are battling addictions are also featured to humanize these issues and help readers better understand that anyone—from young and old, to the wealthy, middle class, or the poor, to those who have a PhD or who are still in high school—can develop toxic relationships with drugs, alcohol, gambling, and/or other behaviors.

The path to detoxing from drugs, alcohol, problem gambling, and other challenges will not be easy—and there may be bumps in the road. But there will be happiness, healing, and the opportunity for personal growth and success for those who continue walking on the road of recovery.

WORDS TO UNDERSTAND

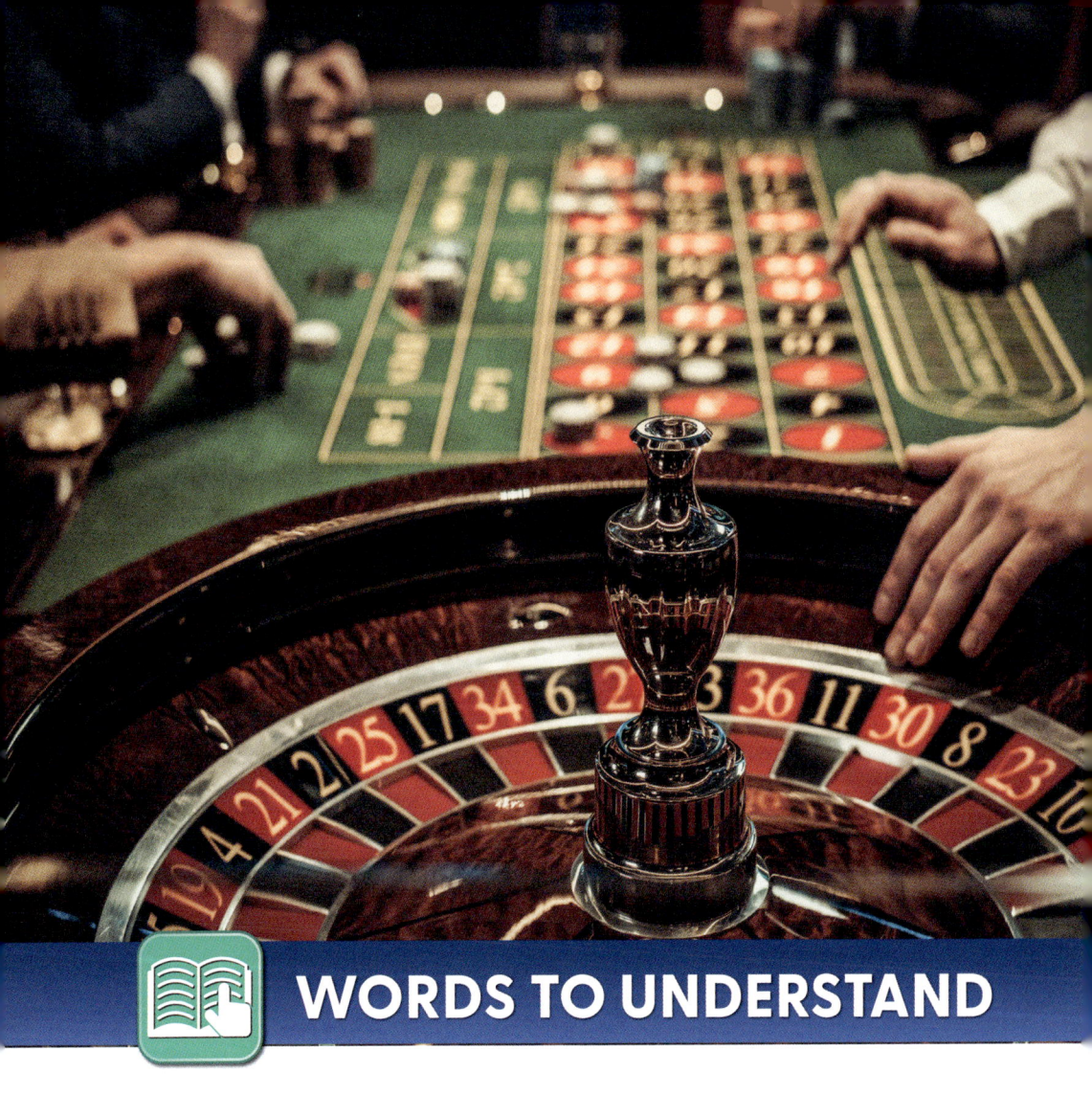

compulsive: referring to actions that are repeated to the point of being an obsession

consequences: negative repercussions caused by a certain action

cricket: a game played with a ball and bat, involving two teams of 11 players each on a large field; the batter defends the wicket, which is similar to home plate in baseball

exacerbated: complicated or made worse by certain actions

proximity: geographical nearness

respite: a break (time away) from a stressful situation

Chapter 1

What Is a Gambling Addiction?

The Dark Side of Gambling

Gambling can be a fun social outing and a great recreational activity. Most people gamble infrequently if at all—perhaps on a vacation or for a special birthday trip—and most people who gamble do so with available money they have, after all bills are paid.

But there is a darker side to gambling. Even infrequent gamblers can become problem gamblers. A problem gambler is someone who becomes addicted to gambling over time. When the person has lost the ability to control their gambling, it has become problematic. Pretty soon, a person may gamble with money that is earmarked for other things, like rent or food. The addiction can become overpowering and all-consuming, creating problems in the person's life.

According to the Mayo Clinic, gambling is classified as an impulse control disorder, one of several mental health disorders in which a person is unable to control impulsive urges. Gambling disorders can cause serious issues in a person's day-to-day life. Gambling becomes an obsession. The gambler is constantly thinking about when he or she can gamble and is likely preoccupied with obtaining the money to

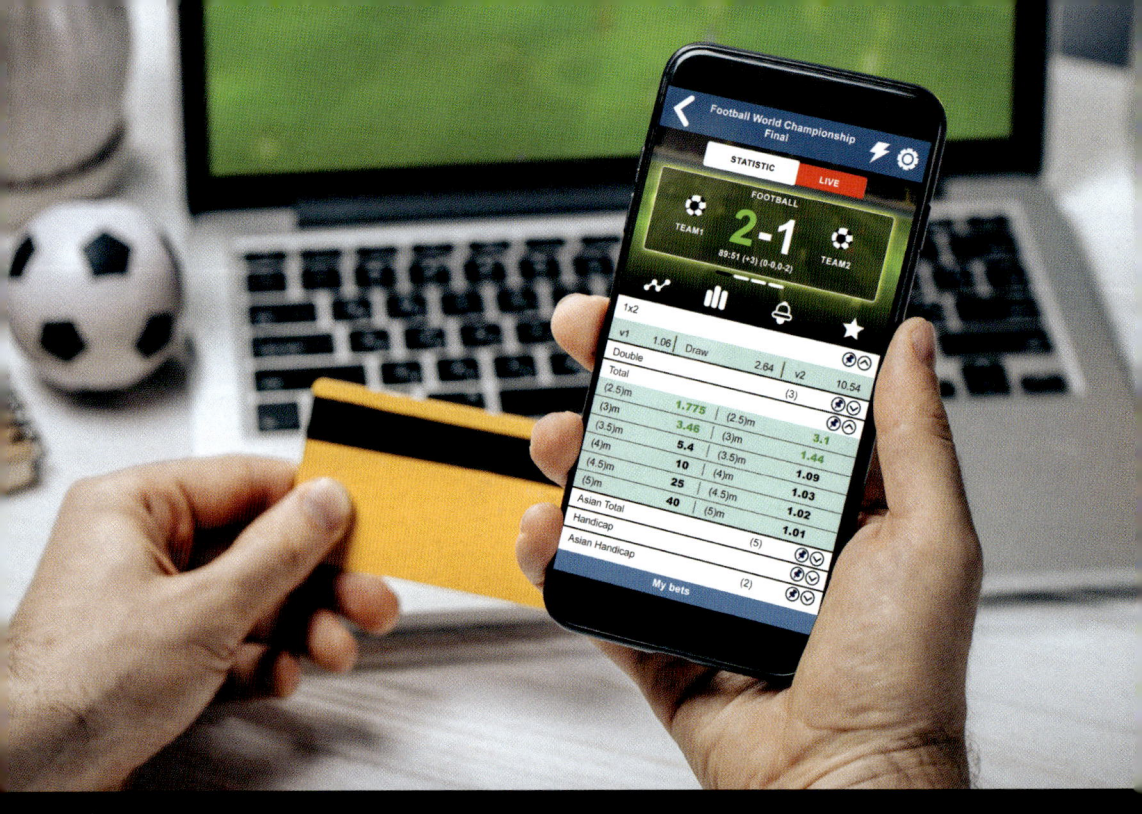

Online gambling is legal in some US states and foreign countries such as Australia, the United Kingdom, France, and New Zealand.

gamble. Gambling addicts can have trouble at work or school and can have strained personal relationships. Many people who are addicted to gambling have financial or even legal problems.

Addictive gambling is also referred to as *gambling disorder* or **compulsive** *gambling*. The person who is addicted often feels uncontrollable urges to gamble, even though the addiction causes issues in their life. People often feel the urge to risk money in the hope of getting more money. A person can very quickly deplete their savings account or even build up great debt.

Similar to drug and alcohol addictions, gambling triggers the brain's reward system, and chemical reactions occur that fuel the addiction. Therefore, gambling is like a substance-based reaction. The brain releases chemicals called *endorphins* when we do something pleasurable, such as eating a favorite food. Gambling can release endorphins, and a person who has low endorphins may like the way he or she feels when gambling. As such, gambling stimulates the brain and its reward system in the same way that it does in drug and alcohol addictions.

Gambling is a brain addiction, because it creates the same chemical changes in the brain as substance abuse. Gamblers experience withdrawal effects and continue to gamble despite negative **consequences**.

Financial problems usually occur as a result with a gambling addiction, but they do not cause the addiction. Rarely does a person turn to gambling simply to make more money. In fact, the root of a gambling problem has little to do with finances. These addictions

People between the ages of 20 and 40 are the age group most likely to develop a gambling addiction.

start at an emotional level, and gambling may represent a temporary **respite** from the pressures and stresses of daily life. The person may initially only gamble on certain occasions, like on a Friday evening after a long week of work, but the problem can soon spin out of control, just like a drug or alcohol addiction. Pretty soon, the gambler may become obsessed with gambling. These addictions are further **exacerbated** by the access to online gambling, which has become much more prevalent in recent years.

Sports betting is the most common form of gambling among students.

Who Becomes Addicted to Gambling?

In the United States, age, gender, and **proximity** to casinos are all determining factors. Men are more than twice as likely to develop a gambling problem as women are. People between the ages of 20 and 40 are the age group most likely to develop a gambling addiction, and many college students develop serious gambling problems while still in school. These students are much more likely to experience depression and anxiety, and they are at higher risk for drug and alcohol abuse.

Finally, the risk of developing a gambling addiction doubles when people live within ten miles of a casino. However, online gambling is very prevalent in society and has greatly increased the problem of addiction because people can gamble in the privacy of their homes.

Families with a compulsive gambler are much more likely to have volatile family situations (that can include physical or emotional abuse), and more than 67 percent of compulsive gamblers will engage in criminal activity, such as theft, that is related to the gambling.

Gambling Statistics in Other Countries

Gambling is not just a problem in the United States. Other countries report serious gambling issues, too. For example, a 2018 paper published in the medical journal *Läkartidningen* noted that gambling is a serious issue in Sweden. Two percent of the nation's population has a problem with gambling, with about 0.4 percent meeting the criteria for gambling disorders. With a population of 10 million people in 2018, this means that 200,000 Swedes have gambling problems. In Sweden, part of the issue is cultural. Gambling is a part of the society, but the problem is becoming a national and public health issue.

Author Marc Valleur discusses gambling in France and states that it is also part of the national culture there. In an article in the medical

It's estimated that 200,000 Swedes have gambling problems.

journal *Addiction,* Valleur explains that the king of France created a royal lottery in 1776 for the people, and gambling has been a staple in the French culture ever since.

Similar to France and other European Union (EU) countries, gambling is part of the Spanish culture, and the gambling industry is one of the fastest-growing sectors in Spain as new technologies are developed for online gambling.

In Germany, gambling is illegal, but slot machines are not classified as gambling, so they are very prevalent in the country. Treatment for gambling has been covered by the country's health plans.

Gambling has an interesting history in the Czech Republic. It was not readily accessible during the communist rule of the country, and citizens have much more access to gambling. After 1989, gambling facilities increased, but the country did not establish many laws to regulate it. Like Sweden, the Czech Republic has about 200,000 people with a gambling problem, and an article in the journal *Addiction* by author Vivek Benegal states that the issue is most prevalent in people aged 15 to 64. Many cities have banned electronic gaming machines to try to help the problem from growing larger.

In China, gambling has been strictly forbidden throughout most of the country's history. Gambling is allowed for entertainment, but money cannot be exchanged. The Chinese public has a high demand for gambling, so national lotteries have been put in place. Chinese culture sees gambling addiction as misconduct rather than a mental disorder, and the country is experiencing a rise in both youth and

The Venetian Casino in Macau.

It's estimated that gamblers spend more than $300 billion each year betting on cricket matches.

illegal gambling. It's noteworthy that gambling is legal in Macau, a special administrative region of China. Gambling and tourism are the two main components of Macau's economy. In fact Macau is one of the world's largest gambling destinations (in terms of gambling revenue).

In India, gambling is very popular and has long been a part of daily life. During the British occupation of India, the British first encouraged gambling, because it brought money to them. However, they began seeing the social problems that it caused, so a law was enacted in 1867, placing a formal ban on most forms of gambling. As a result, India developed a very large illegal gambling market, particularly for sports betting on games like **cricket**.

These countries all say that the increased availability of Internet gaming and casinos and Internet sports betting is a cause for the rise in the problem. For instance, French data shows that online gamblers are much more likely to be addicted than land-based gamblers. In the US, sports betting is legal in 30 states, and 90 percent of it happens online, according to ESPN.com. A recovering addicted gambler might have great difficulty, because online betting is available 24/7 and is accessible by phone. A person can bet on Russian ping pong, Swedish basketball, and so much more. Health experts are seeing a tremendous rise in gambling addictions due to electronic sports betting, also called *esports betting*.

Male vs. Female Gamblers

While men gamble twice as frequently as women, changing social norms have made society more accepting of female gamblers. Research has been conducted regarding the differences between men and women in terms of gambling. Men prefer to play in casinos alone, while women prefer to go to casinos in groups as a social outing. Women tend to prefer games of chance, like slots, keno, and bingo, whereas men tend to prefer games of skill, such as poker or blackjack.

LEARN MORE ABOUT GAMBLING AROUND THE WORLD

In this chapter, several countries' stances on gambling are outlined. Research a different country not mentioned in this chapter. For example, you might choose Australia or New Zealand. Search the Internet for information. Is gambling legal there? How many people in the country have gambling addictions? Is gambling accepted in the culture?

Studies show that women prefer to play games of chance such as slots.

When men and women have a gambling problem, they typically react differently. Men show anger and aggression when losing, while women show sadness and anxiety. Studies show that women who are bored and lonely are much more likely to develop a gambling problem.

Forms of Gambling

Sports betting is by far the most popular form of gambling worldwide. It is also an ancient form of betting. There is evidence of early cavemen betting on fights, but these days, a person can bet on anything, such as a horse race, a dog race, the performance of a player, or a team. Popular betting sports include horseracing, tennis, soccer, and American football. Electronic sports betting even allows someone to bet on a play in real time, such as a touchdown pass or a soccer penalty kick.

In a 2021 paper in the journal *Frontiers in Psychiatry,* researchers from the Pathological Gambling Unit of the Department of Mental Health of the hospital Consorci Sanitari de Terrassa in Spain showed that online sports betting is a very prevalent addiction among youth. They found that younger non-smokers with university-level education and higher weekly income to spend preferred online sports betting to other forms of gambling.

Lotteries are also a form of betting. Spending on lotto tickets adds up to about $1,038 each year per consumer (who choose to purchase the tickets), according to a survey commissioned by Bankrate of more than 2,300 US adults. Lotteries are an easy way to gamble for people

Electronic sports betting generates global revenue of nearly $2 billion each year.

TERRIBLE ODDS

The change of winning a big payoff on a slot machine can be as high as one in 34 million. Machines are set so that you will eventually lose. One common misconception is that your chances of winning increase the longer you play on a slot machine, but in actuality the probability of winning goes down. Keep this in mind when you become old enough to visit a casino.

who do not know how to play games such as poker, blackjack, or roulette in casinos. Lotteries have been around since ancient times and are often legal in countries that do not allow any other form of gambling.

Casino games are probably the most recognized form of gambling worldwide. Players can spin wheels, shoot dice, or play many card games.

Raffles are considered a form of gambling. You have likely participated in a raffle fundraiser for a school, team, or charity. You buy a ticket for a certain price, and if your ticket is selected, you win the big prize. Raffles are games of pure chance.

Some people even consider investing in the stock market to be a form of gambling. After all, buying a stock and hoping it will go up in value could be construed as gambling, because there is always the element of chance.

TEXT-DEPENDENT QUESTIONS

1. Why is gambling considered to be a brain problem?
2. Who is most likely to develop a gambling issue?
3. Why do health professionals consider online gaming a problem?

WORDS TO UNDERSTAND

amassed: gathered together in one location

comorbidity: a condition that exists alongside another condition, such as diabetes and obesity together

pervasive: spreading through every part of something

preoccupied: lost in thought about something else and not present in the current matter

recoup: to try to gain something back

reminisce: to think fondly about a past event

Chapter 2

Signs of a Gambling Disorder

The Tell-Tale Signs of Gambling Addiction

Is it possible to distinguish a person who is just having a fun casino night outing from one with an addiction to gambling? There are tell-tale signs. The biggest sign is that the person is unable to reduce or stop gambling. The person simply cannot control the urge to gamble and may be restless or irritable when not gambling. When most people gamble, they set a dollar limit before going into the casino. Once that money is spent, the casino trip is done. However, an addict may keep spending and spending. Casinos have cash ATM machines, so the person may keep doing bank withdrawals to get more money.

Another sign is that the person is **preoccupied** with gambling. They may constantly talk about gambling, **reminisce** about past gambling experiences, or frequently plan how to obtain more money to gamble. A friend who needs to bet higher and higher amounts of money to get the same thrill from gambling may also have an addiction. The addict may also gamble more and more to **recoup** losses; this is termed "chasing losses." Gambling addicts often lie to family and friends regarding the extent of their gambling but may also frequently ask close family members and friends for a loan or a

Some people are so desperate to gamble that they will steal from their loved ones to fuel their addiction.

bailout because of financial troubles incurred while gambling. They often jeopardize school attendance and grades, a job, or relationship because of gambling. They may even steal money or items to sell to get more money to gamble. Gambling is a fun social activity, but friends who gamble to escape problems or alleviate depression may have already developed a gambling addiction or may be at higher risk for developing one.

Risk Factors

What causes a person to become a compulsive gambler? This form of impulse control disorder is not well understood, but like most addictions it is thought to develop from biological, genetic, and environmental factors. Many people who play cards or place bets will never develop a gambling problem, so why do certain people become addicted to gambling?

Official diagnosis of a gambling behavior is done according to criteria outlined in the *Diagnostic and Statistical Manual of Mental Disorders, 5th Edition* (*DSM-5*). This nearly 1,000-page book is published by the American Psychiatric Association and is the principal authority on psychiatric diagnoses.

According to the *DSM-5,* a person who exhibits at least four of the stated criteria for a twelve-month period has an addiction to gambling. Showing four to five of the criteria is a mild case, six to seven is moderate, and eight to nine indicates a severe addiction. There are several risk factors. Check out a copy of the *DSM-5* at your local library to learn more about these criteria. The following sections provide more information on major risk factors.

What started as casual wagering for Beth turned into a raging addiction that caused financial ruin and jeopardized her relationship with her husband.

STORIES OF ADDICTION

Beth enjoyed going to the casinos with her husband. They went several times a year just to do something different and have fun. Soon, her gambling became a problem. She began to withdraw more and more cash from her account, and pretty soon, she withdrew all that she had available. She lived fairly close to the casino and would lie to her husband about where she was going. Instead, she would say she was shopping, at work, or running other errands. Soon, Beth began charging her credit cards, then her husband's cards. One day, he applied for a new credit card and was denied. He thought it was a mistake because he had always paid his bills on time. He soon learned that Beth had been placing substantial charges on his card and that his credit rating was ruined.

Joaquin became so addicted to gambling that he could not stop. He had thoughts of suicide. He was losing so much money and could not cope with his situation. His family had disowned him, because they couldn't trust him. He stole money from them and lied to them about his gambling.

Kiara has a gambling addiction. For the last six years, she has amassed incredible debt. She also is addicted to alcohol, and the combination of her addictions requires a lot of effort on her part to overcome. She lost her job and her home, and her husband divorced her.

Joseph started out as a shy gambler. He didn't want to gamble in public, so he called bookies on the phone to place his bets. He won a few times, and soon placing bets turned into an addiction that he could not control. He began to spend more time at the racetrack and lost his job. He has severe gambling debts that he cannot repay. He has no cash to pay for basic necessities like food and rent, but he still has the impulse to gamble. He does not know where to turn.

Gambling has taken over Keiko's life. Her husband divorced her, and she had to ask her parents for financial support. Keiko has four children, that she is not properly taking care of. Her parents are elderly and cannot emotionally, physically, or financially support all of them. Keiko recently went to the casino and spent $15,000. At first, she had a winning streak, and she gambled money she didn't have, boldly thinking that she could double or triple her money. This was the last money she had to support her children, and the government might have to step in and remove the children from Keiko.

    Which of these personal stories most resonated with you? Do you know someone with a gambling problem? If so, write down their story, and if not, write a description of what you think it would be like to live with a gambling addiction.

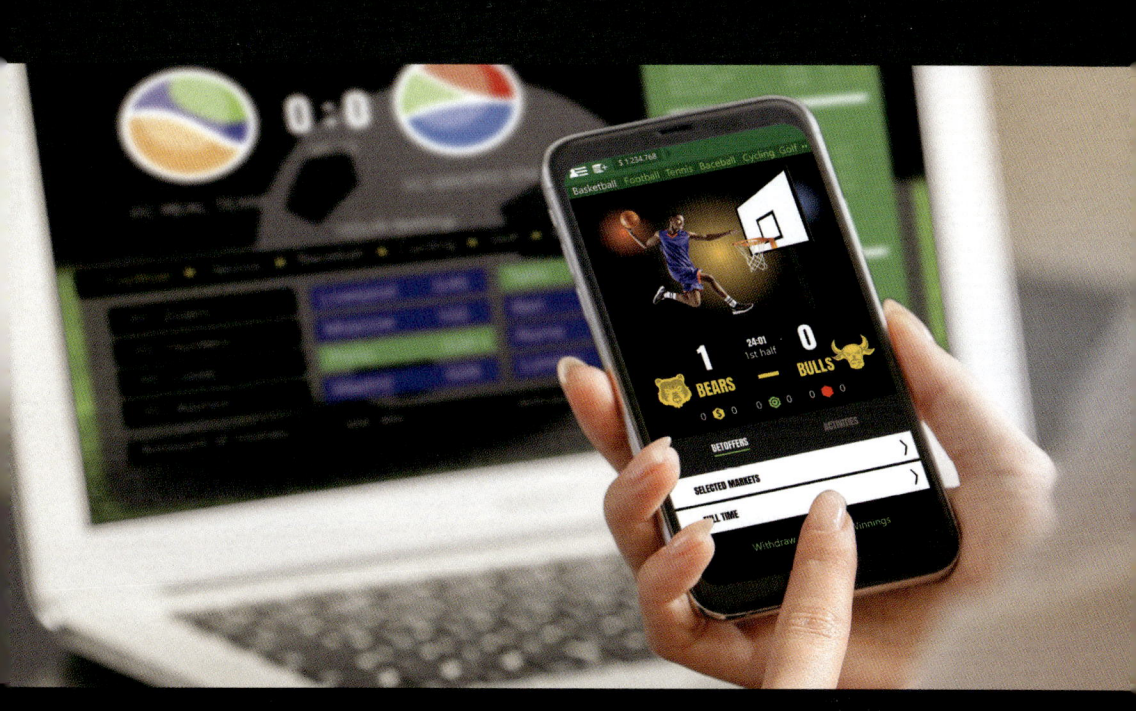

A young person who observes their parents gambling (such as e-wagering on sports at home) is much more likely to develop into a compulsive gambler. Parents should never gamble around their children.

Age and Gender

Younger and middle-aged people (20 to 40 years old) tend to develop compulsive gambling habits more commonly, but the problem is **pervasive** in older adults, too. A person who gambled at a young age, or who observed their parents gambling, is much more likely to develop into a compulsive gambler. If the person has a strong influence to gamble from family and friends, they are more likely to be

Those who are highly competitive and have a win-at-all-costs mindset often have a higher risk of becoming addicted to gambling.

or become a compulsive gambler. Furthermore, compulsive gambling is much more common in men. However, gambling patterns in men and women are becoming more similar as social norms are changing. When women do gamble, they typically start later in life and can become addicted much more rapidly.

Personality

Personality can also be a risk factor. Highly competitive people are much more likely to become addicted to gambling, as are workaholics. People who are easily bored and who are often restless and impulsive are also more likely to develop an addiction.

Comorbidities

Perhaps the biggest indicator of whether someone will develop an addiction to gambling is the presence of another mental health disorder. Compulsive gamblers often have substance abuse problems, such as a drug or alcohol addiction, and may have other psychiatric diseases such as personality disorder, attention deficit hyperactivity disorder (ADHD), bipolar disorder, or obsessive-compulsive disorder (OCD). Having one of these disorders along with a gambling addiction is called **comorbidity** or a *comorbid condition*.

In one paper published in the *Asian Journal of Psychiatry,* 96 percent of gamblers were estimated to have one or more psychiatric disorders, such as substance use disorder, depression, or anxiety. Researchers estimated that 64 percent have three or more psychiatric disorders.

Many problem gamblers have comorbid conditions. Researchers are still studying these coexisting conditions to find possible interventions for these behaviors. Most treatments involve therapies for the gambling addiction, along with proven medications or other therapies for the other disorders. Doctors often start treatment for the most severe disorder first, then follow with other necessary treatments.

Compulsive gamblers often have substance abuse problems, such as alcohol addiction. Alcohol can exacerbate gambling problems, because overindulgence leads to reduced inhibitions and poor decision-making.

COVID-19 and Gambling Addiction

COVID-19 has had a tremendous impact on mental health. Researchers already know that people in isolation have more negative emotions and increase use of substances such as drugs and alcohol. Before the pandemic, gambling was increasingly becoming recognized as a major public health concern, and many researchers published papers about it. The COVID-19 restrictions were a major driver toward people gambling. During the pandemic, betting on esports and fantasy sports skyrocketed, because most physical casinos were shut down. Even if casinos were open, many gamblers did not want to gamble in public, preferring to physically distance. Research published in *Frontiers in Psychiatry* shows a 17.6 percent increase in compulsive gamblers, with many having anxiety disorder as a comorbid condition. Online gambling was not restricted during the pandemic, and companies actually created more online games during that period. Online gambling is riskier because it can be done in secret. For many, gambling is a coping mechanism, and many used it during the lockdown to alleviate isolation and loneliness. Unfortunately for many, the habit has led to further financial instability.

Casino owners do everything possible to encourage gamblers to gamble for as long as possible. They use lighting, sounds, and other features to create an almost narcotic-like effect that encourages gamblers to make risky decisions in the pursuit of winning.

DOES CASINO DESIGN PROMOTE GAMBLING?

Do casinos themselves stimulate people to gamble? Researchers at the University of British Columbia in Canada have shown that the noises and lights in a casino stimulate people to gamble and therefore promote risky gambling behavior. Every casino has loud noises of slot machine jackpots being won, flashing lights, and stimulating music. The researchers showed that these signals create visual and auditory (referring to the hearing system of the body) overload for a person. If a person with a gambling addiction (or a high risk for developing one) even walks through such a casino, these inputs to the brain may be a significant factor in promoting problem gambling. The gamblers in the study were less motivated by the odds of a particular game they wanted to play, and more motivated by the audiovisual features present in the casino. Initial research in lab rats showed that the animals exhibited riskier behaviors when exposed to flashing lights, and researchers wanted to see whether the same was true with humans. In the study, 131 people were given a video gambling game to play. Some played in the quiet, while others played with all the bells and whistles that one would find in a casino. Researchers used eye-tracking technology and observed that people paid less attention to the onscreen information about the odds, and more attention to images of money going across the screen. Players without the audiovisual stimulation made more reserved decisions and lost less money. The brain has a specific area that is responsible for risky activity, and these light and sound cues stimulate that area. The researchers published their work in the *Journal of Neuroscience*.

TEXT-DEPENDENT QUESTIONS

1. What aspects of a casino's design promote gambling?
2. Name two signs that someone may have a gambling problem.
3. What was the impact of COVID-19 on gambling addiction?

WORDS TO UNDERSTAND

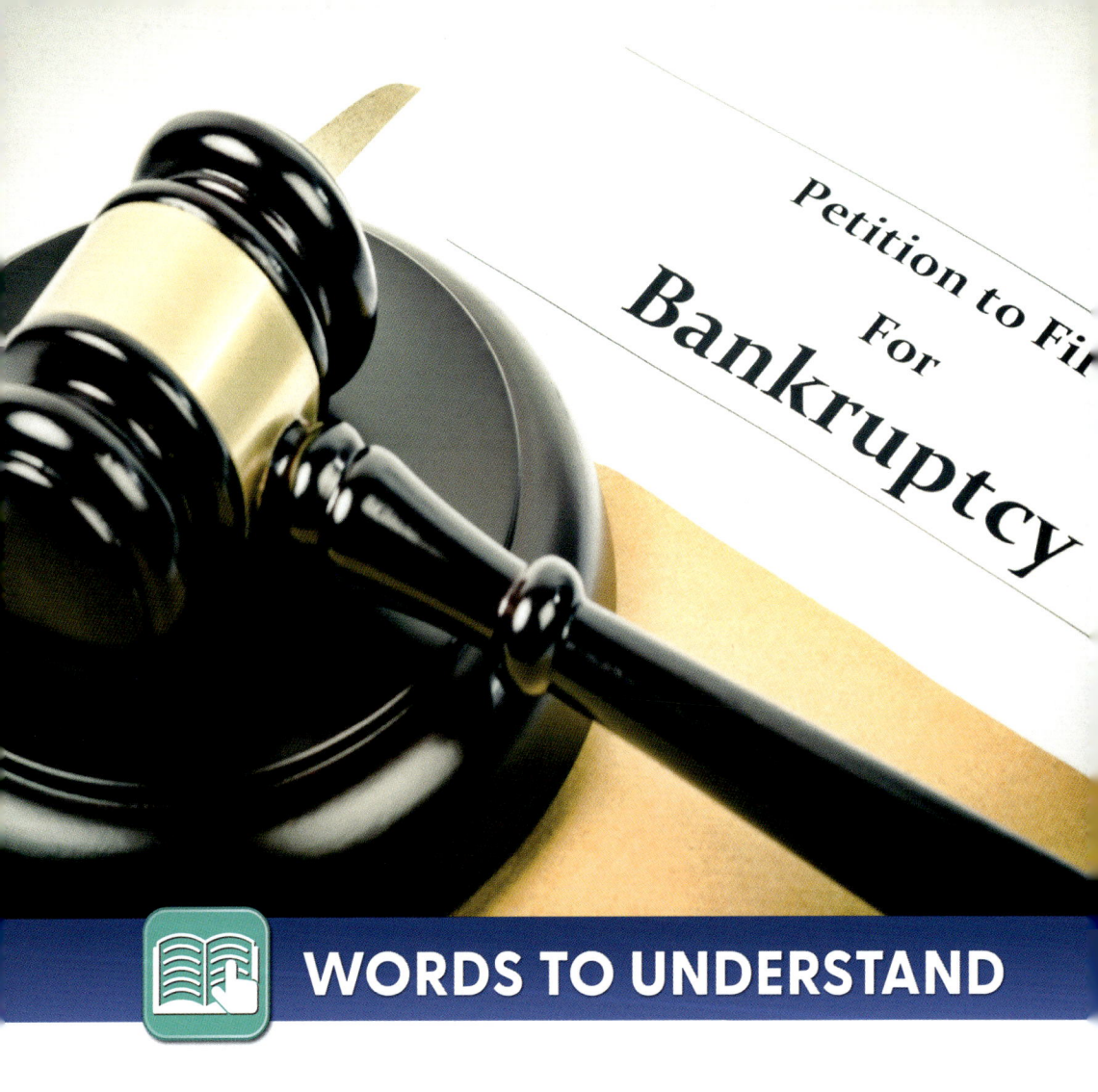

abstinence: discontinuing an activity

domestic abuse: a pattern of physical, emotional, sexual, psychological, or economic threats or actions that are used to gain or maintain power and control over an intimate partner; also known as *domestic violence*

enabler: a person who makes excuses for an addict or who facilitates their addiction

serene: peaceful

silent addiction: an addiction that is hidden from friends, family, and coworkers

Chapter 3

Consequences of Gambling Addiction

Compulsive Gambling = Lifelong Problems

Compulsive gambling can create profound and long-lasting consequences. Addictive gambling is often associated with a reduced quality of life. The person has impaired function and can even be involved in criminal activity. Divorce and rifts in relationships occur more often, and gambling addicts experience high rates of bankruptcy. Gambling problems can occur during the teen years or early adulthood, and males tend to start gambling at a much earlier age than females. Gambling is more accepted as a legitimate and legal form of entertainment, but for a gambling addict, it presents a problem because it is not only more accepted but also more accessible. These problems are explored in this chapter.

Relationship Problems

Quite often, an addict feels that their gambling problem is not affecting anyone else, including their family. They simply don't recognize that the gambling can potentially ruin the lives of people around them. Gamblers don't readily accept reality, and their denial contributes to the problem. The gambler can easily hide

Problem gambling can destroy relationships, because the gambler often drains a family's assets and lies or gets defensive about their gambling problem.

their addiction from coworkers and friends, and many families are embarrassed by the addiction and therefore hide it from others. This is why gambling addiction is often called a **silent addiction**. Spouses of gambling addicts deal with severe psychological and emotional stress, but they also may experience financial, social, and legal issues. These consequences put a lot of pressure on a relationship, and many marriages simply don't survive.

Here are some stories from spouses.
Ann: My husband was a closet gambler with a silent gambling addiction. I didn't even know about it. He was a loving husband and father, and over time turned into a shell of a person with empty eyes. He could barely function to drag himself into work each day. He began sneaking around and lying to me and the kids, and his boss. Everyone lost respect for him. I wondered which one of us would first have a nervous breakdown. I wanted to divorce him, and I even thought about committing suicide. I even wished he would die so the gambling issue would go away.

Jim: I spent 24 years dealing with my wife's gambling addiction. Our lives were an emotional and financial mess. She hid her addiction from everyone except me. All our friends thought she was so wonderful, and I was tired of cleaning up her messes, both emotional and financial. I no longer trusted her.

Mary: My husband Jake recently relapsed after six years of **abstinence** from gambling, and it made me both sad and mad. While he did not attend our Gamblers Anonymous (GA) meetings, I continued, and decided to work on myself instead of concentrating on his addiction. I became more self-confident and tried to live one day at a time. I always had the hope that he would return to the GA meetings with me, and one day he just did. I don't know why. I never nagged him or

Mary stuck by her husband, Jake, during his gambling relapse and credits her perseverance and the support offered by Gamblers Anonymous as keys to helping him recover and rebuild their relationship.

begged him to. Later, he admitted that he probably would not have returned to GA if I had not kept going. We have been attending for the last three years together, and our relationship is much closer. We live a **serene** life.

Rafael: I am active in the gay community in my city, and that is how I met my partner, Tomas. We traveled together, and when we went to Lake Tahoe and visited several casinos, I became aware that he had a gambling problem. I attended GA meetings, but he wouldn't. He stopped gambling after I had attended about four meetings, and I thought it was no longer a problem, but within a year, Tomas had started gambling again. His gambling is much worse now, and I feel

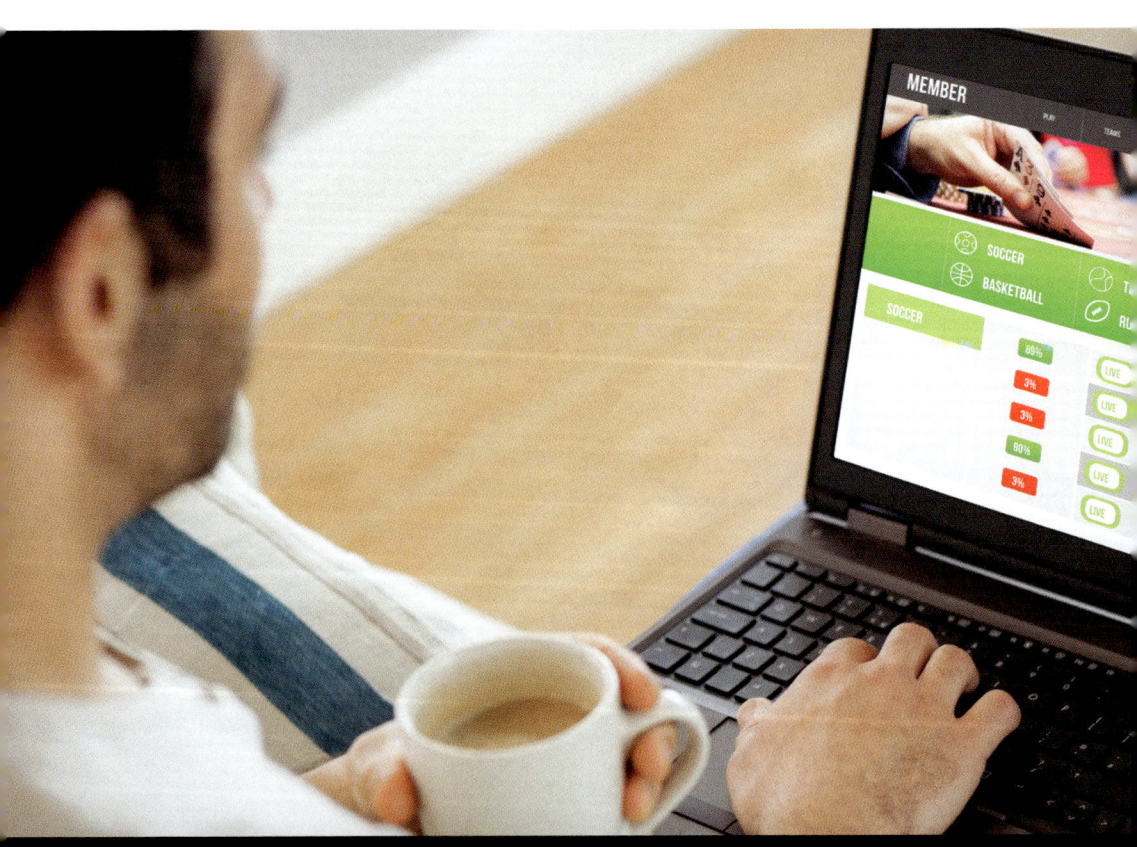

The availability of online gambling makes it easier for problem gamblers to lie to their loved ones about their activities. They can say they are working on their laptops but, instead, may be spending hours wagering online.

like I am drowning. He still won't go to meetings with me, but I keep going because they help. Pretty soon, I am going to be at the point where I need to make a decision whether to stay or leave. I love him, and I don't want to leave, but it is becoming too hard to deal with, and I deserve more out of life.

Families and friends of gamblers often experience significant stress and tension. Spouses, parents, children, siblings, and friends can all be affected.

Gambling addicts lie. This is the territory for any compulsion. The gambler assures a friend who loans him money that he will pay it back right away and then avoids the friend when it is time to pay up. Addicts want to go to casinos for long periods of time. If they do so in secret, they will lie and say they are going to work or somewhere else. Many spouses have thought their significant other was at work, only to find that he or she had lost their job and had been spending all the time at the casino. If the person is honest about going to the casino, he or she will manipulate or even threaten the family to get to go gambling.

As these relationship problems occur, the person often closes himself in, going deeper into isolation to avoid the shame of seeing anyone close to him or her. As this happens, a spouse may carry the load that the gambler is not handling. Over time, the spouse is resentful. He or she also tends to keep feelings inside, because they are too embarrassed to talk to anyone about what is really going on. Some spouses and parents simply cannot face the fact that their loved one has a gambling addiction; they became **enablers** of the situation, making excuses about the gambling and treating it as normal.

Children are particularly affected by parents who have gambling addictions. The parents can't provide the child with a sense of security, and the child has no confidence in what the parents tell him or her. These children often grow to have significant anxieties and apprehensions. A child can usually sense a problem even though the

KEISHA'S STORY

My child is a compulsive gambler. There, I said it. For years, I knew it but wasn't able to admit it. I was frustrated, ashamed, and lonely. I made excuses for him, saying he was gambling just to blow off steam after a big test or to get out and have some fun after a relationship breakup. When he was in college and came home for the Christmas holidays, I might not see him for two whole days. He would stay at the casino for twenty hours straight sometimes. I made excuses, telling my friends he was at a friend's house. When he graduated from college and got his first job, I was happy. I said nothing to him about the addiction, hoping it would go away. He lost that first job when his gambling spiraled out of control, and he got himself into severe financial difficulty. He was sad to lose the job of his dreams, but that prompted him to go to GA meetings. I went with him and still do. We find the GA meetings to be a warm safe place to listen and be listened to. I know that I did not cause the gambling problem, so I don't feel guilty.

parents have not talked to them about the issue. Children overhear arguments and see that parents might be sleeping separately. The child may also know about the money problems. Many children will begin to act out both at home and in school, because they feel insecure in the family unit. Many children develop psychological issues such as depression, fear, and anxiety.

Sadly, **domestic abuse** occurs more frequently in families with a gambling addict. The financial pressures and emotional issues are often very high, and arguments can easily get out of hand and result in violence toward the spouse or child. The gambler may experience a bad losing streak and take it out on the family once he or she gets home. Partners often either seek help for the person or walk away from the relationship, particularly if the addict is not ready for the help. For safety reasons, the family needs to leave in this situation.

Financial and Legal Problems

Bob's story: I was 45 years old. I was very successful in my job and one of the youngest to reach my corporate executive title. I was absorbed in my work, and my marriage suffered. My wife abruptly divorced me, and I began to gamble because I was bored and lonely. I hadn't gambled much before, because I never had the time. I liked it—a little too much. I started out with a lot of money, so I was able to gamble for years without seeing any financial consequences. Over time, I overcharged on my credit cards, and my money eventually ran out. The bank

Constant arguments between parents regarding gambling or other addictions can be extremely damaging to young children.

MAGDALENA'S STORY

I grew up with a father who was a compulsive gambler. My mother enabled his gambling. Our family was completely dysfunctional. There was never time to care for each other and share with each other. Sometimes, I couldn't even get a hug when I needed it. I married early at age 18, just to get out of the house, but I couldn't provide for my husband physically or emotionally. Finally, after ten years of a stressful marriage, I found out that he, too, was a compulsive gambler. Looking back, I realize that I acted just like my mom did, enabling the situation for ten years. I am currently in counseling and working hard to educate my children about the dangers of gambling.

foreclosed on my house. I was homeless with barely enough money to live on. My work performance deteriorated, and I was fired from my job. I lost everything I had put into my career for twenty years, but I got severance pay, and I spent it all on gambling. I don't take care of myself, and my health is deteriorating but I am too embarrassed to get help, because I don't want people to see how far I have fallen.

Bob's story is very common. Most people with gambling addictions experience severe financial issues. In fact, financial issues are often the first sign that someone has a gambling problem. The person may start asking friends for money to pay overdue bills. A spouse may not even realize that her significant other has a gambling problem, but the overdue bills that come through are likely a clue. If the gambling becomes uncontrollable, the person may spend even more money trying to win back casino losses, but that just plunges them deeper into debt.

Clues that someone has a gambling problem include maxed-out credit cards, overdue bills, and requests to friends and family for money. Despite the person's adequate income, he or she may have problems paying for basic necessities like food, clothing, and rent. The person always seems short of money. Many gamblers pull all their money from savings or retirement accounts, or they pawn items to get cash. They take cash advances from their paychecks and may take out loans. They may invest in very risky stocks. Gamblers think money is the solution to their gambling problem and that everything will be fixed once they get the "big win."

Gambling addicts can have property like automobiles repossessed by the bank and can have a home foreclosure. Once their debt becomes too large, the person may have to go through voluntary

It might be hard to believe, but there are many true stories of wealthy people who literally went from "riches" to "rags" and living on the street because of their gambling addiction.

bankruptcy, which is a serious step only to be considered after you get professional advice.

Suicide

Problem gamblers are much more likely to attempt suicide, according to several research studies. The shame of losing money and creating financial hardship for the family is sometimes too much to bear. GambleAware, a non-profit organization in the United Kingdom, commissioned a research study that found gamblers were six times more likely to entertain thoughts of suicide and fifteen times more likely to commit suicide than people without a gambling addiction.

BILL'S STORY

Bill was from a loving Asian family. He worked in the family business, his father's equipment-rental shop, and saved significant money for college. He lived at home and attended college. On the weekends, Bill played poker with his buddies, but they didn't have much money to bet. A casino opened nearby his home when Bill turned 21. Being of legal age, he was excited to visit the casino. He spent all of his savings on gambling and soon began to ask friends for money. When they didn't have money to loan, he stole money from his father's business. His father could not figure out who was stealing from him, and he never suspected Bill. Soon, his gambling habit became $12,000 a month. His parents urged him to go to a ten-day treatment center, but Bill did not complete the treatment. Shortly thereafter, Bill's father realized that Bill had been stealing from him and kicked him out of the business. Bill shot himself a week later.

This chapter has focused on the stories of people who are struggling with an addiction to gambling. It's important to know that there is help available and that many people are able to put their gambling addiction behind them and repair broken relationships.

PROBLEM GAMBLING AWARENESS MONTH

March is Problem Gambling Awareness Month and represents a good time to discuss the stigma surrounding this mental health issue. This addiction can have devastating results on careers, families, and relationships. It is important to discuss these issues so they can be dealt with early.

Depression, financial problems, and substance abuse might drive their suicidal thoughts. In the study, nearly one in five people (19 percent) had considered suicide within the last year. By comparison, about 4 percent of the general population considers suicide. Quite often, the burden falls to the family to intervene in the addict's life to get help. It is very stressful and can put a strain on the family, but remember that there are resources out there to help.

Learn more about Problem Gambling Awareness Month.

48   Detoxing from Gambling

TEXT-DEPENDENT QUESTIONS

1. Name three signs that someone may be having financial difficulty due to gambling debts.
2. What is a banned list?
3. Why is an interventionalist important?

WORDS TO UNDERSTAND

destructive: having the potential to hurt and destroy
notarized: officially certified by an approved authority who authenticates signatures on important documents
pharmacological: referring to the use of drugs as a therapy
psychological: relating to the mind and brain

Chapter 4

Preventing and Treating Gambling Addictions

Knowing When to Seek Help

Compulsive gamblers cannot limit their gambling and therefore develop a pattern of **destructive** behavior that becomes worse over time. Many struggle with the decision of when to see a doctor. When does the gambling problem become severe enough to seek treatment? It is complicated by the fact that compulsive gamblers can enter a period of remission when they gamble less often or not at all. However, the remission usually won't last without treatment.

Many gamblers will be in denial that they have a problem. In fact, denial is almost always a factor when someone has an addictive or compulsive behavior, and family and friends often struggle with whether to confront the person. If you do have a gambling issue, and family members and friends have expressed concern, listen to their worries.

Many problem gamblers deny that they have a problem despite clear evidence their excessive wagering is damaging relationships and the financial stability of their families.

Tests

There are tests and evaluations that you can use or that doctors or therapists can apply to diagnose compulsive gambling. For example, the organization Gamblers Anonymous uses a 20-question survey to help with diagnosis. A few sample questions include Did you ever lose time from work or school due to gambling?, After a win, did you have a strong urge to return and win more? Did you often gamble until all your money was gone?, Have you ever felt remorse after gambling?, and Have you ever committed, or considered committing, an illegal act to finance gambling? The complete list of questions can be found at www.gamblersanonymous.org/ga/content/20-questions and are listed below.

The above questions are based on the South Oaks Gambling Screen (SOGS; Lesieur & Blume, 1987) 20-item questionnaire that was based on *DSM-3* criteria, which were updated in *DSM-5*. The SOGS can

SIGNS THAT SOMEONE HAS A GAMBLING ADDICTION

- Constant preoccupation with gambling
- A need to gamble with more and more money to get the same thrill
- Inability to control their gambling
- Feeling irritable when they can't gamble
- Use of gambling to alleviate stress or escape problems
- Trying to recoup money lost by gambling more
- Lying to family and friends about how much or how often they gamble
- Damaging important relationships or work or school performance because of gambling
- Stealing to get gambling money
- Asking others for money to fix their financial trouble caused by gambling

Remember that if you have at least four of these symptoms, according to the *DSM-5*, you likely have a gambling addiction. If you do, try your hardest to avoid gambling in any form, and avoid hanging around with people who like to gamble or in places where gambling occurs. Early testing and treatment are very important in keeping the gambling issue from worsening.

A therapist conducts an assessment to determine whether her patient has a gambling addiction.

be self-administered or administered by professionals, but these days professionals most often utilize the *DSM-5* criteria. Questionnaires such as the SOGS are good, because they offer a convenient way to screen general populations for compulsive gambling. A similar questionnaire is the Problem Gambling Severity Index (PGSI, Ferris & Wynne, 2001), a self-reporting tool designed to help individuals determine their own at-risk behaviors with respect to gambling habits over the last year. (The PGSI is based on the longer Canadian Problem Gambling Index.) The PGSI survey has nine questions, with possible answers and correlating scores of Never (0), Sometimes (1), Most of the Time (2), or Almost Always (3). The higher the score, the more likely the person has a gambling addiction. The questions in the survey are:

In the last 12 months:
1. Have you gambled more than you could afford to lose?
2. Have you felt the need to gamble with larger amounts of money to get the same feeling of excitement?

3. When you have gambled and lost, did you go back another day to try to win back the money you lost?
4. Have you borrowed money or sold something in order to have money to gamble?
5. Have you felt like you might have a problem with gambling?
6. Has gambling caused you any health problems (including stress, anxiety etc.)?
7. Have people criticized your betting or told you that you have a problem, regardless of if you thought it was true?
8. Has your gambling caused any financial problems for you or your household?
9. Have you felt guilty about the way you gamble or what happens when you gamble?

Have you ever sold personal property, such as jewelry, so that you could gamble? If so, you might have a gambling problem.

Once all questions have been answered, add up the score. A score of zero (0) indicates a person who can gamble with no negative consequences. A score of 1 to 2 indicates a low-risk gambler who might have a few issues but no lasting addiction or negative consequences. A score of 3 to 7 indicates a gambler at moderate risk of developing addiction, while a score of 8 or more does indicate a problem gambler. The PGSI is for personal use and is rarely used by doctors for diagnosis in a clinical setting. Criteria from the *DSM-5* are used in a clinical setting.

Treatment Options and Other Strategies

Families often wonder what they can do to help a person with a gambling problem. Seeking treatment from professionals is recommended, but families can do their part. The following sections provide information on treatment options and other strategies that are used to help people heal and stop problem gambling.

A problem gambler provides advice to help people stop addictive gambling behaviors.

SUPER BOWL BETTING

Mental health experts warn that the wide availability of betting on the Super Bowl can lead people to a gambling addiction. In many states and around the world, gamblers can place online bets for the game. Multiple bets can be made, such as betting on the score at the end of each quarter, whether players get hurt, and real-time betting on completion of plays.

An estimated 31 million Americans bet on the 2022 Super Bowl game between the Cincinnati Bengals and the Los Angeles Rams, according to the American Gaming Association. The availability of gaming apps has made it easy to place bets from a cell phone. It only takes a few seconds. Sports experts estimated that Americans bet a total of $7.6 billion on the 2022 Super Bowl. Mental health experts say that the accessibility of online gaming makes the situation much more dangerous for at-risk people.

Modeling Good Behavior

Social modeling is important. People model the behaviors of influential people with whom they spend a lot of time. Parents are big influences, as are grandparents and other relatives like siblings, friends, teachers, and coaches. People with a gambling addiction will use the behaviors of others as a guide, so if you suspect someone has a gambling issue, do not take them to a casino or engage in online gambling with them. Find other social activities that do not involve this risky behavior.

Support Groups

Support groups are great ways to get support for oneself or for family or friends to suggest help. Gamblers Anonymous (GA) is one

If you have a loved one with a gambling problem, try to participate in activities—such as hiking—that remove them from triggers like easy access to casinos and the Internet (i.e., online gambling).

such group. It offers a 12-Step program adopted from Alcoholics Anonymous (AA). While many local, state, national, and global support groups exist, GA is the oldest and most recognized. The group was started in 1957 by two men who had an obsession to gamble. As they met regularly, neither returned to gambling, and they expanded the group to other members. The premise of the group is that certain changes must occur in the person to prevent a relapse into gambling.

The 12-Step program was first developed by AA and has been adopted worldwide for all types of addictions. The 12 steps outline a plan for overcoming addictions and compulsions. In the support groups, people help each other to follow these steps and abstain from gambling. According to data from the Substance Abuse and Mental Health Services Administration national survey, about 75 percent of all treatment centers use some form of a 12-Step program.

GA offers in-person meetings and began virtual meetings during the COVID-19 pandemic. It offers online support and information and many other services. Learn more:

Gamblers Anonymous
(909) 931-9056
isomain@gamblersanonymous.org
www.gamblersanonymous.org

SMART Recovery is another useful resource. It is a nationwide, non-profit organization that offers free support groups to those who desire to gain independence from any type of addictive behavior.

ALCOHOLICS ANONYMOUS ORIGINAL 12 STEPS

1. Admitting powerlessness over the addiction
2. Believing that a higher power (in whatever form) can help
3. Deciding to turn control over to the higher power
4. Taking a personal inventory
5. Admitting to the higher power, oneself, and another person the wrongs done
6. Being ready to have the higher power correct any shortcomings in one's character
7. Asking the higher power to remove those shortcomings
8. Making a list of wrongs done to others and being willing to make amends for those wrongs
9. Contacting those who have been hurt, unless doing so would harm the person
10. Continuing to take personal inventory and admitting when one is wrong
11. Seeking enlightenment and connection with the higher power via prayer and meditation
12. Carrying the message of the 12 Steps to others in need

It also has a free Internet Message Board discussion group and recovery-related publications for sale. Learn more:
SMART Recovery
(440) 951-5357
www.smartrecovery.org

Cognitive Behavioral Therapy

Most addictions, including a gambling addiction, greatly benefit from professional therapy. Cognitive behavioral therapy (CBT) has been shown to be very effective for gambling addiction. CBT helps people learn to problem-solve. It explores relationships between the feelings and thoughts about gambling and the behaviors that follow. CBT teaches the addict that their perceptions about gambling directly influence how they respond with behaviors. In other words, thought

Support groups—for both problem gamblers and their loved ones—are excellent resources to help people recover from their gambling addiction.

processes inform actions and behaviors. CBT refers to a group of therapies and can include rational emotive behavior therapy and dialectical behavior therapy, both of which are described below.

CBT is grounded in the philosophy that a person will act based on how they perceive events. For example, a belief that everything will be bad today will cause the person to make decisions that influence the day to turn out in a negative way. The person also blocks thoughts or actions that could be positive. In the end, the person's belief is reinforced when nothing goes right that day. People with these thoughts often get trapped in a vicious and negative cycle of events.

CBT helps a person adjust their thoughts so that emotion and behavior are influenced in a different way. This process is called *cognitive restructuring*. Generally, a person's thinking pattern is established in childhood. If a parent or teacher focuses on the child only when he or she fails, they can influence the formation of certain thoughts. The person can view the world in extremes like black or white and nothing in between, or feel excessive responsibility for every bad thing that can happen. These patterns can create anxiety, and a person might gamble to alleviate that anxiety.

People in CBT are guided on how to unlearn these negative reactions and learn positive new ones. They learn how to positively react to challenging situations and learn to break down overwhelming problems into small and manageable parts. CBT therapists usually help the person set short and reachable goals at first to progress through the therapy. Over time, the person gradually changes how he or she feels and thinks in a tough situation. These changes in attitudes and behaviors help people address their gambling addiction.

CBT is not just sitting and talking to a therapist. It is a structured approach that keeps both people focused on goals for each session. People can reveal sensitive issues, and the therapist helps the person understand the issues. The gambler may be encouraged to keep a journal about his or her experiences, and the therapist can teach

Although it might seem daunting, those who are addicted to drugs can recover and lead happy and productive lives.

relaxation techniques and mindfulness. What is mindfulness? It involves teaching a person how to be more aware of his or her own physical, mental, and emotional state in the present moment. The individual learns how to pay attention to their experiences and the feelings, thoughts, and bodily reactions they cause.

In CBT therapy, the person might have to read assignments and write essays about thoughts and feelings. He or she might have to learn thinking exercises. Time must be made outside of the therapy session to complete homework, which has the added benefit of keeping the person engaged and working on their own to help address their addiction.

Rational Emotive Behavior Therapy
Rational emotive behavior therapy (REBT) is one form of CBT that helps people learn to manage thoughts and emotions in a more realistic way. REBT is used with success for obsessive-compulsive

disorders, and since gambling addiction is a compulsion, REBT has been effective as well. In fact, many athletes use REBT to overcome irrational thoughts about sports competitions and their own performance. The Olympic champion swimmer Michael Phelps talks often about how therapy has helped him achieve success.

Clinicians describe REBT as an action-oriented approach designed to help people manage irrational beliefs about themselves and the world. The goal of the therapy is to have people let go of negative beliefs and replace them with positive ones to overcome their addiction. Most people blame external events for unhappiness, and REBT teaches the person that it is their interpretation of these events that lies at the heart of most **psychological** issues. REBT uses the ABC model:

- A is an activating event that happens in your environment
- B is your belief and thoughts about the event
- C is the consequence of your emotional response to the belief

During REBT sessions, the therapist helps the person to apply the ABC model to daily life events. For example, if you are having a relationship conflict, the therapist will talk to you about what event triggered the problem, why you feel depressed about it, and the consequences of actions you did or did not take in regard to the initial conflict. You will be encouraged to identify the beliefs that led to your negative feelings and then work to change those beliefs to have a healthier emotional response to the conflict. Many people with addictions feel that they have no control over their own happiness and that joy comes from external sources. REBT teaches the person that he or she is indeed in control of these things and that joy comes from within. However, holding unyielding beliefs makes it nearly impossible to find that joy, so REBT teaches a person to change his or her beliefs to a healthier version.

Above all, REBT teaches a person that they are worthy of acceptance (and self-acceptance) regardless of the struggles and mistakes caused by their gambling addiction.

Dialectical Behavior Therapy

Dialectical behavior therapy (DBT) is another form of CBT that teaches people how to cope with stress, live in the moment, and improve relationships. DBT was originally developed as a treatment for borderline personality disorder (BPD), but it has been shown to help with addictions like gambling and is also effective for post-traumatic stress disorder (PTSD).

DBT is used in both individual and group therapy sessions and can also be used in phone coaching sessions between a therapist and patient. This therapy uses several core strategies. The first is development of mindfulness skills to focus on the present (the "live in the moment" approach). DBT also teaches people how to better tolerate distress and crisis handling. Finally, DBT teaches a person better interpersonal effectiveness on how to function better in relationships, learn to say "no" to things, and become more assertive in expressing their needs. It also teaches the addict how to better deal with challenging people and how to more effectively communicate and listen.

Exposure Therapy

Exposure therapy is a psychological treatment that helps people confront fears. The therapy is designed to create a safe environment in which to expose the person to his or her fears to help reduce them over the long term.

Exposure therapy has been effective for obsessive-compulsive disorder, and more recently it has been used to treat people with gambling addiction. The person experiences graded exposure to gambling situations and learns responses to prevent gambling. The foundation of the therapy is that in order not to gamble, the person must learn how to resist urges and cues to gamble in certain situations. As exposure to gambling increases, and the person learns not to place bets in those situations, their urge to gamble diminishes over time. After the urge to gamble has gone, secondary measures like avoiding gambling establishments, not carrying cash, and others are reinforced.

Pharmacological Agents

Pharmacological agents are medications used to treat compulsive gambling. Certain antidepressants and mood stabilizers have been used with mixed success in reducing gambling behavior. Medications are given typically when a person has another disorder like depression or ADHD that goes along with the gambling addiction, and they have been used less frequently to treat gambling addiction by itself. Other medications, called *narcotic (opioid) antagonists* and *serotonin reuptake inhibitors* may also help people who are compulsive gamblers.

Interventions

People with addiction problems often don't get help until someone pushes them to do so, and family members are often the ones who must intervene. When someone has an addiction, an intervention may be an effective way to address the issue. Interventions are usually done as a last resort, so the family is often very stressed, and emotions are high. It is important to have a licensed professional interventionalist conduct the session. They know how to start it and keep it going, and they know how to address hostility from the addict. It is important to not push the addict further away, and the interventionalist knows how to accomplish this. Interventions are an act of love, but the addict does not always see it that way. Still, the large majority of interventions (87 percent), according to Scripps Health, result in the admission of the person to a treatment center. While the 87 percent refers to all addictions, interventions are important for gambling addiction as well.

Interventions are emotional and tense. People must choose words wisely to ensure the addicted person realizes you are approaching this from a perspective of love and concern as the reason you are pushing him or her to get help. Some family members find it too difficult to attend in person, so they write a letter to the gambling addict. Letters should be affectionate but should stick to the facts about the problem the addiction causes. Tell the person how the addiction has affected their health and how it has affected you.

The family often has to issue an ultimatum to the gambler, meaning that if he or she does not get help and treatment, there will be a set of consequences, but the family will still be there to support the person in treatment and recovery. Nevertheless, it is still important to let the person know that they are valuable to the family who loves them and believes in them. However, the person also needs to know how worried the family is.

The interventionalist will likely prepare a script for each family member. Be prepared to give the person space, and listen to what he or she has to say. The family must expect resistance, but the interventionalist will provide solutions for the excuses and denial that will likely be expressed.

An intervention may be the only way that loved ones can get through to a person who has a gambling or other type of addiction.

EXPLORATION ACTIVITY

Design an intervention. It might be for someone you know, or you might just design one that you think would be effective. Who would be there? Who wouldn't attend? What would you say or not say? What would be your main goal for the session?

There are certain things not to do during an intervention. Don't make excuses for the addiction. The person needs to understand how disruptive and upsetting the problem is. Don't use foul language, harsh words, or name-calling, and make sure you have a calm tone of voice. Avoid anger; you are trying to reason with the person. The interventionalist may exclude family members who have a negative relationship with the person or who may not be able to control negative behaviors during the intervention. Spend just as much or more time discussing solutions; don't focus all the time on the problem.

Placement on a Banned List

Remember that compulsive gamblers cannot limit their own behaviors, so family and friends may have to step in to encourage them to place themselves on a banned list. A person with a gambling addiction can be asked to be placed on a banned list (which is also known as a *self-exclusion list),* which blocks them from being allowed to visit a casino. Once the person's name is on the list, the gambler is prohibited from entering the casino or using any of its services, such as ATM machines or online gambling. Each state has a department of gaming where the form is available. The form will likely need to be **notarized**, and a current photo of the person must be provided. You can set up a meeting with the state office, and you will meet with a self-exclusion administrator who can explain the program details. Many of these offices have a notary and equipment to take a photo of the person. Most appointments need to be scheduled in advance. Requirements vary by state, but most need information such as the person's name, address, and contact information as well as descriptive information, such as age, weight, height, gender, and race. A person can be banned in one or all states, and different types of activity, such as in-person gambling, online gambling, and use of ATM machines, can be banned. However, the gambler must provide permission to be banned and sign voluntarily; a person cannot sign for them. The banning period is usually not less than twelve months but can be implemented for the remainder of the person's life. After the minimum 12-month period, the gambler must request removal from the list, or else he or she will remain on it. Individuals who initially requested a lifetime ban cannot be removed from the list under any circumstances.

Final Thoughts

Regardless of the treatments and strategies that are used, remember that all efforts must begin with the addict's recognition of their gambling problem. Compulsive gamblers often deny a problem, so it is left up to those around them to suggest treatment. Gambling is a long-term disorder, just like other addictions, and it tends to get worse without treatment. A person may seem to recover from the gambling addiction, only to relapse. However, with love and support, and the right treatment, it is possible to recover from addictive gambling.

TEXT-DEPENDENT QUESTIONS

1. Why is modeling good behavior so important in someone's recovery from a gambling addiction?
2. Name a type of therapy that is effective for gambling addiction. Why do you think this therapy is effective?
3. Why are support groups effective in helping someone who has an addiction?

GLOSSARY OF KEY TERMS

12-step program: This program was first developed by the Alcoholics Anonymous support group and has been adopted worldwide for all types of addictions, including gambling. The 12 steps outline a plan for overcoming addictions and compulsions.

abstinence: Discontinuing an activity that might cause a person harm. Gamblers often abstain from gambling for a period of time but will begin gambling obsessively again without treatment.

auditory cues: The auditory system is the anatomy of the ear that allows a person to hear. Casinos are designed with loud bells and whistles (i.e., auditory cues) that have been scientifically proven to encourage risky behavior.

bankruptcy: Gamblers often incur so much debt that their property is seized by creditors in bankruptcy court.

banned list: All 50 states have a way to put a gambler on the banned list, which is also known as self-exclusion list. Being placed on the list bans the person from physically being present in the casino, getting cash from ATM machines at the casino, participating in online gambling that is available through the casino, and from using any other casino services.

cognitive behavioral therapy (CBT): CBT has been shown to be a very effective treatment for gambling addictions. It helps people learn how to problem-solve. It explores relationships between the feelings and thoughts about gambling and the behaviors that follow. CBT teaches the addict that their perceptions about gambling directly influence how they respond with behaviors. In other words, thought processes inform actions and behaviors. CBT refers to a group of therapies.

comorbidity: A condition that exists alongside another condition, such as diabetes and obesity together. Many people with a gambling addiction also have another mental health disease such as anxiety, depression, or obsessive-compulsive disorder.

compartmentalize: To separate into isolated categories. Gamblers often live their life in compartments, meaning they function normally at work and have a gambling addiction in their private life away from work. They may lie to their spouse about their gambling, further compartmentalizing their lives.

compulsion: An action that is repeated over and over again.

consequences: Negative repercussions of a certain action.

detrimental: Something that causes injury or damage. Gambling addiction has negative emotional and financial effects.

dialectical behavior therapy (DBT): DBT is a form of cognitive behavioral therapy (CBT) that teaches people how to cope with stress, live in the moment, and improve relationships. It was originally developed as a treatment for borderline personality disorder, but it has been shown to help with addictions like gambling and is also effective for treating post-traumatic stress disorder (PTSD).

dopamine: A neurotransmitter chemical in the brain that is released as part of the brain's reward system.

enabler: A person who makes excuses for an addict or who facilitates their addiction.

foreclosure: A legal proceeding that removes a homeowner's right to the mortgage on the house; banks foreclose on homes when gamblers cannot make their house payments.

impulse control disorder: One of several mental health disorders in which a person is unable to control impulsive urges.

influential: Referring to a person or experience that has a strong effect or influence (positive or negative) on someone's life. People with parents who had a gambling addiction are very likely to also develop the same addiction in their teen or early adult years.

interventionalist: A medical or social/psychological professional who assists with an intervention to confront someone about their gambling or other addiction. When family members feel that a person's gambling is out of control, and the person cannot quit gambling on his or her own, an intervention can help.

mindfulness: The process of becoming more aware of one's own physical, mental, and emotional state in the present moment. The individual learns how to pay attention to experiences and the feelings, thoughts, and body reactions they cause.

GLOSSARY OF KEY TERMS

nonpharmacological: Referring to nondrug therapies such as behavioral therapies and interventions.

perpetuate: To continue something or keep it going. Gamblers perpetuate their gambling to recoup their losses in hopes of winning a big jackpot to make up for all the past money they have lost.

pharmacological: Referring to the use of drugs as a therapy.

problem gambler: Someone who becomes addicted to gambling over time and who has lost the ability to control their gambling.

psychological: Relating to the mind and brain.

rational emotive behavior therapy (REBT): One form of cognitive-based therapy. It helps people learn to manage thoughts and emotions in a more realistic way. REBT is used with success for obsessive-compulsive disorder, and since gambling addiction is a compulsion, REBT has been effective as well.

rationalize: To explain or justify something as being normal even though it is not; gamblers often rationalize.

relapse: A recurrence of an issue after experiencing some improvement.

recoup: To regroup or try to gain something back. Gamblers often try to recoup their losses, hoping for the big win.

reminisce: To think fondly about a past event. One sign of a gambling disorder is a person's reminiscence about a past gambling event or a preoccupation with everything that involves gambling.

remission: Something that has been relieved or canceled. The term is often used to explain a decline of cancer, but gamblers can often be in a remission period where they do not gamble for a period of time.

respite: A break (time away) from a stressful situation.

silent addiction: An addiction that is hidden from friends, family, and coworkers. Gambling is a silent addiction, because it is easy to hide from coworkers, family, and friends

social modeling: Children and teens model the behaviors of influential people such as parents, other relatives, and teachers with whom they spend a lot of time. Parents are big influencers, as are grandparents and other relatives such as siblings, friends, teachers, and coaches. People with a gambling addiction will use the behavior of others as a guide, so if you suspect that someone has a gambling issue, do not take them to a casino or engage in online gambling with them. Find other social activities that do not involve this risky behavior.

support groups: Therapy and discussion groups that provide a gambler with support. They also provide support services to family and friends of the person who has a gambling problem. Gamblers Anonymous is one example of a support group that offers in-person, online, and phone support.

trauma: Severe psychological distress that results from an event or series of events that are emotionally disturbing or even life-threatening. The person has lasting effects and trouble functioning in a mental, social, emotional, or even physical way. Examples of trauma can be sexual abuse, childhood neglect, or living with a substance use disorder.

ultimatum: A final demand for something to change. During an intervention, a family may give a compulsive gambler an ultimatum to quit gambling or suffer repercussions such as divorce or cutting off financial support.

FURTHER READING

Cook, James. *The Gambling Addiction Recovery Book: Working the Twelve of Steps of Gamblers Anonymous & Steps for Meetings*. Allen, TX: G.A. Publishing: 2020.

Dahl, Kurt. *Gambling Addiction*. Independently Published, 2020.

Durham, Steve, and Kathryn Hashimoto. *The History of Gambling in America*. Hoboken, NJ: Pearson, 2019.

Schüll, Natasha Dow. *Addiction by Design: Machine Gambling in Las Vegas*. Princeton, NJ: Princeton University Press, 2014.

INTERNET RESOURCES

www.mayoclinic.org/diseases-conditions/compulsive-gambling/symptoms-causes/syc-20355178: This resource from the Mayo Clinic provides information on the symptoms and causes of compulsive gambling, as well as treatment options.

https://oasas.ny.gov/problem-gambling: This website from the New York State Office of Addiction Services and Supports provides a list of warning signs for problem gambling and suggests ways to prevent problem gambling and how to play responsibly.

www.espn.com/chalk/story/_/id/33237601/inside-life-gambling-help-line-worker: This article provides a deep look inside the life of a gambling help line worker.

www.goodtherapy.org: Millions of people use GoodTherapy to find therapists and counselors, rehab and residential treatment centers, and mental health resources.

INDEX

A
AA (Alcoholics Anonymous), 58–59, 70
ABC model, 63
abstinence, 36, 39, 70
abuse. *See specific types of abuse*
Addiction, 16–17
Addiction by Design (Schüll), 74
addictions, 7, 9, 26. *See also* gambling addiction
ADHD (attention deficit hyperactivity disorder), 31, 65
admitting powerlessness, 59
adolescents, 14, 17, 21, 29–30
age, 15, 30–31
aggression, 20
alcohol addiction
    discussion, 7, 9, 15, 28
    gamblers and, 31–32
    similarities with gambling, 12–14
Alcoholics Anonymous (AA), 58–59, 70
American football, 20
American Gaming Association, 57
American Psychiatric Association, 27
American Psychological Association (APA), 7
anger, 20, 67
antidepressants, 65
anxiety
    comorbidities, 31–32, 70
    discussion, 15, 20, 42, 55, 61
APA (American Psychological Association), 7
arguing, 42–43
Asian Journal of Psychiatry, 31
athletes, 63
ATM machines, 25, 67–68, 70
attention deficit hyperactivity disorder (ADHD), 31, 65
auditory cues, 34, 70
Australia, 12, 19

B
Bankrate, 21
bankruptcy, 36–37, 46, 70
banned lists, 67–68, 70
baseball, 10
beliefs, 63
Benegal, Vivek, 17
betting, 26, 28, 57, 64
bingo, 19
biological factors, 26. *See also specific biological factors*
bipolar disorder, 31
blackjack, 19, 22
borderline personality disorder (BPD), 64, 71
brain, 12–13, 34, 71

C
Canada, 34
Canadian Problem Gambling Index, 54
card games, 22, 26

casinos. *See also* stories
    ATM machines and, 25
    banned lists and, 67–68, 70
    COVID-19 pandemic and, 32
    design of, 33–34, 70
    discussion, 17–18, 22, 41, 57–58
    male vs. female gamblers, 19
    proximity to, 15, 46
CBT (cognitive behavioral therapy), 60–64, 70
Centers for Disease Control and Prevention (CDC), 7
chemicals, 12–13, 71
children
    discussion, 29, 44, 73
    parents' influence on, 29, 41–43, 61
China, 17–18
Cincinnati Bengals, 57
clinicians, 9
clues, 44–45
coaches, 57, 73
cognitive behavioral therapy (CBT), 60–64, 70
cognitive restructuring, 61
comorbidities, 24, 31–32, 70
compartmentalizing, 70
competitiveness, 30
compulsions, 50, 58, 70, 72
compulsive gambling. *See* gambling addiction
confidence, lack of, 41
Consorci Sanitari Hospital, 21
Cook, James, 74
counselors, 9, 74
COVID-19 pandemic, 7, 32–33, 58
coworkers, 36, 38, 72
credit cards, 28, 43–44
cricket, 10, 18
criminal activity, 15, 37
culture, 15–16
Czech Republic, 16–17

D
Dahl, Kurt, 74
DBT (dialectical behavior therapy), 61, 64, 71
debts, 12, 28, 70
denial, 37, 51–52, 66, 68
Department of Mental Health (Spain), 21
depression
    comorbidities and, 31, 70
    discussion, 15, 26, 42, 48, 65
destructive behavior, 50–51
detoxing, 9. *See also* treatment
diabetes, 24, 70
diagnosis, 52–56
Diagnostic and Statistical Manual of Mental Disorders, 3rd Edition (DSM-3), 52
Diagnostic and Statistical Manual of Mental Disorders, 5th Edition (DSM-5), 27, 52–54, 56
dialectical behavior therapy (DBT), 61, 64, 71
dice, 22

Index **75**

INDEX

disorders. *See specific disorders*
divorce, 37, 73. *See also* stories
doctors, 31, 56
dog races, 20
domestic abuse, 36, 42
dopamine, 71
drugs
    addiction to, 7, 9, 31
    discussion, 12–15
DSM-3 *(Diagnostic and Statistical Manual of Mental Disorders,* 3rd Edition), 52
DSM-5 *(Diagnostic and Statistical Manual of Mental Disorders,* 5th Edition), 27, 52–54, 56
Durham, Steve, 74
dysfunctional family, 44

E
electronic sports betting, 19–21, 32
embarrassment, 38, 41, 44
emotional abuse, 15
enablers, 36, 41, 71
endorphins, 12–13
environment, 26
ESPN.com, 19
esports betting, 19–21, 32
European Union (EU) countries, 16
evaluations, 52–56
excuses, 42, 66–67, 71
exposure therapy, 64–65

F
family members. *See also* stories
    discussion, 42–44, 48, 51
    effect on, 25–26, 37, 41
    help from, 57–58, 65–68
    influence from, 29–31
    lying to, 25, 38, 53, 70
fears, 42, 64
fentanyl, 7
financial problems. *See also* stories
    discussion, 12–13, 27, 38, 42
    sign of addiction, 44, 53, 55
    suicide and, 46, 48
food addiction, 9
football, 20
foreclosure, 28, 43, 45, 71
France, 12, 15–16, 19
friends
    discussion, 44, 51
    effect on, 25–26, 41
    help from, 57–58, 67–68
    influence from, 30–31
    lying to, 25, 53, 70
Frontiers in Psychiatry, 21, 32

G
GambleAware, 46

Gamblers Anonymous (GA)
    discussion, 39–40, 42, 52, 70
    support groups and, 57–59, 73
gambling addiction. *See also* stories
    casino design and, 33–34
    COVID-19 pandemic and, 32–33
    discussion, 7, 9, 31, 68
    factors, 15, 26–27, 30–31
    financial and legal problems, 43–46
    forms of, 20–22
    male vs. female gamblers, 19–20
    negative effects of, 11–14
    in other countries, 15–19
    relationship problems, 37–38, 41–43
    signs of, 25–26, 53
    suicide and, 46, 48
Gambling Addiction (Dahl), 74
Gambling Addiction Recovery Book, The (Cook), 74
gambling help line worker, 74
games
    discussion, 33, 57
    types of, 18–20, 22
gender, 15, 30–31
genetics, 26
Germany, 16
GoodTherapy, 74
grandparents, 57, 73
guilt, 55

H
happiness, 9, 63
Hashimoto, Kathryn, 74
health. *See also mental health*; treatment
    discussion, 15–16, 55, 66
    experts, 19, 21
help. *See also* treatment
    discussion, 9, 43–44, 47–48
    from friends and family, 57–58, 65–68
higher power, 59
hiking, 58
history, 20
History of Gambling in America, The (Durham & Hashimoto), 74
home loss, 28, 43, 45, 71
horseracing, 20

I
impulse control disorder, 11, 26, 71
India, 18
inhibitions, 32
Internet gambling
    accessibility of, 14, 57
    banned lists and, 67–68, 70
    COVID-19 pandemic and, 33
    discussion, 12, 15–16, 19, 21
    lying and, 40
    modeling and, 57, 73

Internet Message Board, 60
interventions, 65–67, 71
investing, 22, 45
irritability, 53
isolation, 32–33, 41

J
job loss, 7, 28, 41–42, 44
journaling, 61
Journal of Neuroscience, 34
joy, 63

K
keno, 19

L
Läkartidningen, 15
legal considerations. *See also* stories
    discussion, 12, 19, 22, 37
    financial problems, 43–46
    legal problems, 12, 38, 43–44
    in other countries, 12, 16–18
letters, 66
loans, 25, 41, 45
loneliness, 33
Los Angeles Rams, 57
lotteries, 16–17, 21–22
love, 65, 68
lying
    discussion, 40–41
    to family and friends, 25, 28, 38, 53, 70

M
Macau, 17–18
Mayo Clinic, 11, 74
medication, 31, 65
meditation, 59
men, 15, 19–20, 31
mental health. *See also* treatment
discussion, 7, 9, 32, 48, 57
disorders, 11, 17, 31, 62, 71
mindfulness, 62, 64, 71
modeling, 57, 72

N
narcotics, 7, 65
New York State Office of Addiction Services and Supports, 74
New Zealand, 12, 19
noise, 33–34

O
obesity, 24, 70
obsession, 11, 14
obsessive-compulsive disorder (OCD), 31, 62, 64, 70, 72
odds, 22, 34
online gambling
    accessibility of, 14, 57
    banned lists and, 67–68, 70
    COVID-19 pandemic and, 33
    discussion, 12, 15–16, 19, 21

    lying and, 40
    modeling and, 57, 73
opioids, 7, 65
overdoses, 7

P
pandemic, 7, 32–33, 58
parents
    effect on children, 29–30, 41–43, 61
    help from, 57–58, 73
Pathological Gambling Unit (Spain), 21
penalty kicks, 20
perceptions, 60–61, 70
personal inventory, 59
personality disorder, 31
personality traits, 30–31
PGSI (Problem Gambling Severity Index), 54–56
pharmacological agents, 65
Phelps, Michael, 63
phone betting, 19, 28, 57
physical abuse, 15
poker, 19, 22, 46
post-traumatic stress disorder (PTSD), 64, 71
prayer, 59
preoccupation, 24–25, 53
problem gamblers, 12, 40, 46, 52, 72. *See also* gambling addiction
Problem Gambling Awareness Month, 48
Problem Gambling Severity Index (PGSI), 54–56
problem-solving, 60, 70
psychiatric disorders, 11, 31, 62, 71
psychiatrists, 9
psychologists, 9
PTSD (post-traumatic stress disorder), 64, 71

R
raffles, 22
rational emotive behavior therapy (REBT), 61–63, 72
rationalizing, 72
rats, 34
recognition, 37, 68
recouping, 24–25, 53, 72
relapses, 39, 58, 68, 72
relationships. *See also* stories
    discussion, 9, 12, 26–27, 53
    interventions and, 65–67
    problems in, 37–38, 41–43
    therapies and, 60, 63–64
relaxation techniques, 62
reminiscing, 24–25, 72
remission period, 51, 72
remorse, 52
respite, 10, 14, 72
roulette, 22
royal lottery, 16

S
sadness, 20
savings, 12, 45–46

INDEX

school
    discussion, 15, 22, 42
    effect on, 12, 26, 52–53
Schüll, Natasha Dow, 74
Scripps Health, 65
self-exclusion list, 67–68, 70
serotonin reuptake inhibitors, 65
sexual abuse, 73
shopping addiction, 9
silent addiction, 36, 38, 72
slot machines, 16, 19–20, 22, 34
SMART Recovery, 59–60
soccer, 20
social media addiction, 7, 9
social modeling, 57, 72
South Oaks Gambling Screen (SOGS), 52, 54
Spain, 16, 21
sports betting
    discussion, 18–21
    Super Bowl, 56–57
    youths and students, 14, 21
spouses
    discussion, 41–42, 44, 70
    husbands, 27–29, 44
    stories from, 38–41
    wives, 39
statistics
    discussion, 7, 13, 15, 31–32
    interventions, 65
    in other countries, 15–19
    suicide, 48
    support groups, 58
stealing, 26, 28, 46, 53
stock market, 22
stories
    of addiction, 27–29
    from children, 44
    discussion, 9, 45–47, 74
    of financial problems, 43–44
    from parents, 42
    from spouses, 38–41
stress
    discussion, 7, 38, 41, 53, 55
    sources of, 7, 9
    therapies and, 64, 71
students, 14–15
substance abuse, 31–32, 48
Substance Abuse and Mental Health Services Administration, 58
substance-based reaction, 12
substance use disorder, 31
suicidal thoughts, 28, 38, 46, 48
Super Bowl, 56–57

support
    discussion, 29, 39, 66, 68
    groups, 57–60, 73
surveys
    discussion, 21, 58
    used for diagnosis, 52–56
Sweden, 15, 17

T
teachers, 57, 61, 73
tennis, 20
tests, 52–56
therapies
    cognitive behavioral therapy, 60–64, 70
    discussion, 31, 50, 74
    exposure therapy, 64–65
therapists, 52, 54, 74
thinking patterns, 60–63
thrills, 25, 53
touchdowns, 20
trauma, 73
treatment
    banned lists, 67–68, 70
    centers, 46, 65, 74
    cognitive behavioral therapy, 60–64, 70
    diagnosis, 52–56
    discussion, 16, 31, 51, 56, 68
    exposure therapy, 64–65
    interventions, 65–67, 71
    pharmacological agents, 65
    social modeling, 57, 72
    support groups, 57–60, 73
12-Step program, 58–59, 70

U
ultimatums, 66, 73
United Kingdom, 12, 46
University of British Columbia, 34
urges
    discussion, 52, 64, 71
    inability to control, 11–12, 25

V
Valleur, Marc, 15–16
Venetian Casino, 17
video game addiction, 7, 9
violence, 36, 42

W
wheels, 22
withdrawal, 13
women, 15, 19–20, 31
workaholics, 31

Y
youths, 14, 17, 21, 29–30

CREDITS

Cover: © s.sermram/Shutterstock; © Anton27/Shutterstock
Page 6: Netfalls Remy Musser, Shutterstock
Page 8: Heder Zambrano, Shutterstock
Page 10: Nejron Photo, Shutterstock
Page 12: Wpadington, Shutterstock
Page 13: PR Image Factory, Shutterstock.
Page 14: Nick, Shutterstock
Page 16: Zuzana Habekova, Shutterstock
Page 17: Benny Marty, Shutterstock
Page 18: Nigel Parker, Shutterstock
Page 20: ALPA PROD, Shutterstock
Page 21: 1455947291, Shutterstock
Page 24: ALPA PROD, Shutterstock
Page 26: YAKOBCHUK VIACHESLAV, Shutterstock
Page 27: RomanR, Shutterstock
Page 29: Pixel-Shot, Shutterstock
Page 30: Dean Drobot, Shutterstock
Page 32: Anton27, Shutterstock
Page 33: Yevgen Belich, Shutterstock
Page 36: PENpics Studio, Shutterstock
Page 38: Rido, Shutterstock
Page 39: Billion Photos, Shutterstock
Page 40: wavebreakmedia, Shutterstock
Page 43: Hananeko Studio, Shutterstock
Page 45: Hananeko Studio, Shutterstock
Page 47: Evgeny Atamanenko, Shutterstock
Page 50: Monkey Business Images, Shutterstock
Page 52: WAYHOME studio, Shutterstock
Page 54: Prostock-studio, Shutterstock
Page 55: Miriam Doerr Martin Frommherz, Shutterstock
Page 58: Monkey Business Images, Shutterstock
Page 60: fizkes, Shutterstock
Page 62: Air Images, Shutterstock
Page 66: Photographee.eu, Shutterstock

AUTHOR'S BIOGRAPHY

Jacqueline Havelka is a rocket scientist turned writer. She is a biomedical engineer trained at Texas A&M University. She worked at Lockheed Martin as an aerospace contractor for the NASA Johnson Space Center in Houston, Texas. In her 25-year career, she managed space life sciences experiments and data for the International Space Station and space shuttle program. She began work on shuttle mission STS-40, and worked until the last shuttle launch of STS-135. While at NASA, she served in both technical lead and management roles. She was a charter designer of the NASA Life Sciences Data Archive, a repository of NASA human, animal, and biological research from the Gemini program to the present day.

In 2017, Havelka founded her own company, Inform Scientific, to provide medical and technical freelance writing. She always had the desire to start her own business, and she loves the challenge and diversity of the international projects that her business brings. She learns something new every single day, and that is a very good thing.